Gift of Pat Dennehey

LIFEWATCH

The Mystery of Nature

EGG TO ROBIN

Oliver S. Owen

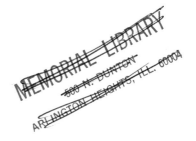

Published by Abdo & Daughters, 4940 Viking Drive, Suite 622, Edina, Minnesota 55435.

Library bound edition distributed by Rockbottom Books, Pentagon Tower, P.O. Box 36036, Minneapolis, Minnesota 55435.

Printed in the United States.

Cover Photo credit: Stock Market
Interior Photo credits: Natural Selection: pages, 5-8, 10-13, 17-19, 22, 27
Stock Market: pages, 9, 14, 15, 16, 21, 23-25

Edited By: Bob Italia

LIBRARY OF CONGRESS CATALOGING-IN-PUBLICATION DATA

Owen, Oliver S., 1920-
  Egg to Robin / Oliver S. Owen.
    p. cm. -- (Lifewatch)
  Includes bibliographical references (p. 29), glossary, and index.
  ISBN 1-56239-293-X
  1. Robins--Life cycles--Juvenile literature. [1. Robins. 2. Birds]
  I. Title. II. Series.
  QL696.P288094 1994
  598.8'42--dc20   94-7793
                      CIP
                      AC

Contents

The Robin

The robin is the most popular songbird in the United States. Wisconsin, Michigan and Connecticut have selected it as their official State Bird. Why is the robin so popular? It likes to live near people. It appears to be a happy and friendly bird. Its song is beautiful. The singing bird seems to say: "Cheerily-cheer-cheer-cheerily." And when it shows up in the northern states, people know that spring has come.

The robin is about ten inches long. It has an orange-red breast, a grayish-brown back and its head is dark. If you get close you can see a white ring around the eye. Have you often wondered how to tell the male from the female? It's easy. The back of the male's head is black. The back of the female's is grayish-black.

In this photo you can see the orange-red breast of the robin and the white ring around the eye.

Most robins live only about 18 months. Rarely do they get older than five years. The oldest known wild robin was 11 years old. A robin kept in a scientist's laboratory lived 17 years!

Are you going to take a trip with your parents soon? Look for robins. They are found throughout the North American continent. In summer they can be found in northern Alaska and Canada. Its cheery song can be heard in any state in the United States during some time of the year. Robins are even found in the hot deserts of Mexico. Many homeowners plant cherry, apple, and mountain ash trees. The robins feast on their fruit. They even build nests in their branches.

Robins eat the fruit of many trees.

Nest Building

The female builds the nest without help from the male. She flies around from one tree to another, looking for a good site. She often chooses a fork in the branch of a tree about six to nine feet from the ground. She will crouch in this fork, spin her body around and around, then start looking for nest materials. She gathers soft mud, weed stalks, tiny twigs, dried grasses, little roots and small leaves. All these are found in nature. But she also collects materials made by humans. She might use old candy bar wrappers. She might collect short pieces of fishing line. Or she might gather tiny bits of cloth.

Female robins work very hard building their nest.

The female robin uses the mud to hold these materials together. She molds the nest into the shape of a cup. She does this while the mud is still soft. She presses against the mud with her breast. Then she turns around many times. This is how the nest gets its cup-like shape. Finally, she lines the nest with dry grasses. She finishes the nest in about six days., By that time she is very tired. After all, she made more than a hundred trips looking for nest materials!

The nest is important to the robin. After all it is where the baby robins are born.

Some nests are built in strange places. A few are built on the ground. Some robins build their nests on top of mail boxes. Others are placed above the busy front door of a house. Some robins even build their nests on ferry boats or cranes.

This robin built her nest inside a barn.

Eggs and Incubation

Once the nest is finished, the female lays eggs, often around sunrise. One egg is laid each day for several days in a row. A robin will lay from three to six eggs. The eggs are oval and one-third the size of a chicken egg.

The female robin lays one egg a day,
usually at sunrise.

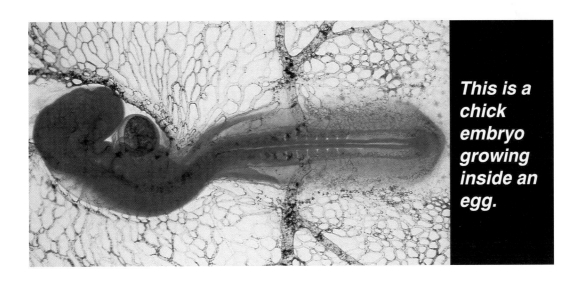

This is a chick embryo growing inside an egg.

The inside of the egg has a yellow part called the yolk. At the top of the yolk is a very tiny spot. This is the embryo which will become a chick. The embryo "feeds" on the yolk. As the embryo gets bigger, the yolk gets smaller. The female gets very hungry while she is "sitting" on the eggs. So she will fly off and feed on a few earthworms. About ten minutes later she flies back to her eggs.

A robin's favorite food is the earthworm.

The mother robin must keep her eggs warm. She does this by pressing her fluffy breast against the eggs. This is called incubation. If the eggs cooled off, the tiny embryo inside the egg would die.

The male robin spends a lot of time near the nest, singing. This tells other robins that he is in charge of that area. He watches for enemies. Raccoons, opossums, squirrels, snakes, blue jays, crows and hawks like eggs for their breakfast. If these egg-eaters get too close to the nest the male robin will get excited. He will jerk his tail up and down. He will make loud warning notes. Then he will fly straight at the animals trying to eat the eggs. This will sometimes chase them away. Sometimes, however, it doesn't.

The male robin sings to protect his territory.

Male robins often take flight to warn off enemies.

Hatching

The newly hatched robins are called nestlings. Nestlings are naked, blind and helpless. The mother must keep them warm. This is called brooding. As the days pass the chick begins to grow tiny feathers. The chick opens its eyes for the first time when it is seven days old. Its feathers gradually grow larger and help keep it warm.

The robin chick works very hard to hatch from the egg.

The newborn robin cries helplessly for food.

The nestlings are tiny—only several inches long. But they have very big appetites. They have a lot of growing to do. So they need a lot of food. Most of this feeding is done by the male. He may make more than a hundred "grocery-shopping" trips each day. Among the "groceries" are spiders, grasshoppers, crickets, June bugs, and earthworms. The nestlings also get their "salad" in the form of clover leaves and grasses. A robin nestling may eat half its weight in food per day.

These nestlings are completely helpless. They can't see or fly and don't have any feathers.

As the nestlings get older, their behavior changes. By the time they are ten days old, they show fear for the first time. They will crouch low in the nest when a hawk screams, or when a house cat starts climbing up the nest tree. However, the greatest killer of baby robins is the weather. A sudden cold spell in May could kill thousands. So could a wind or rain storm.

These nestlings are growing up. They can see and have feathers, but the male robin still has to feed them.

The Young Just Out of the Nest

The young robin leaves its nest when it is about 14 days old. That's because its parents no longer feed it, and it gets very hungry. The young robin looks much like its parents. But it is much smaller and it has dark spots on its breast. That's how we know it belongs to the thrush family. All thrushes have spotted breasts sometime during their life.

These young robins are preparing to leave the nest.

This young robin is on its own.

The parents don't have to teach the young robins how to fly. The young bird does well the very first time. Some may fly more than 100 yards when they first leave their nest. During the first few days out of the nest the young robins beg for food with high-pitched calls. They keep close to the parent bird who feeds them. When the parent bird finds a worm and holds it in its bill, the young robin rushes to get fed.

Soon the young robin must find food for itself. It must learn where to find shelter from wind and rain storms. It must learn how to "talk" to other robins. And it must learn how to escape from its enemies: the house cat, raccoons, foxes, hawks, owls and humans. Humans do a lot of harm to young robins. They may take a young bird into the house and try to make a pet out of it. Sadly, most of these young robins will get sick and die.

*Once the young robin is on its own it learns
quickly how to take care of itself.*

The Fully Grown Robin

The young robin grows rapidly. By the time it is five months old it is fully grown—about ten inches long. In September it gets a new set of feathers. The spots on the breast are gone. The tail has grown longer. The young robin looks much like its parents.

A robin grows quickly, sprouting new feathers and a new tail. Its breast becomes bright orange.

In the fall, robins eat more food than ever. They must store up fat under their skin. This is the "fuel" which will power them on a long flight to the South. This flight is called a migration. Why do they fly south? To escape the cold and to find food. After all, how may earthworms have you seen in a snowdrift lately?

This young robin has stored fat under its skin for its long flight south.

The young robin does not migrate alone. It joins other robins to form big flocks. These birds stay together during the flight south. They migrate mainly at night. They may move 50 to 100 miles each night. Finally they arrive at their winter home. It may be in the southern United States. It may even be in Mexico. The robin flock stays together all winter. At the end of February, some robins begin their spring migration. Many return to where they were hatched. The male robins migrate ahead of the females. When they arrive at their northern home, they set up a territory. It is a one-half acre area which is defended against other robins.

When male robins return home they set up territory in a place with plenty of food and protection.

A territory has all the things a robin needs. It has plenty of worms and other food. It has a tree where the robin can sing. It has a place to build a nest. It has thick shrubs where the robin can find shelter from wind and rain. And it is where the robin will find his mate.

The male robin defends his territory only against other male robins. He will crouch and lift up his tail. He will fluff out his feathers so that he will look bigger. Then he might make a short run at the intruder and peck him with his bill.

Once the male establishes the territory the female robin begins to build the nest.

The female robins arrive in the North several days after the males. The males recognize the females by the gray color of their heads. A young male will fly to the female. If the female already has a mate, she will ignore the singing male. If she does not have a mate she may be attracted to the male's singing. She will stay inside his territory and accept him as her mate. Soon the female will build a nest and lay eggs. And this is where our story began! We have followed the robin's life from egg to adult robin and back to egg. An amazing story, don't you think?

Robins take their mates in the spring.

Glossary

Egg tooth   sharp tooth on top of the baby bird's bill which is used to crack the egg shell.

Embryo   baby bird inside the egg.

Habitat   natural home of an animal.

Incubate   mother bird keeping eggs warm with her breast.

Migration   flight of robin to its winter or summer home.

Nestling   young bird on the nest.

Territory   an area which is defended.

Bibliography

Gill, Frank B. *Ornithology*. New York: W. H. Freeman, 1989.

Harrison, Hal H. *A Field Guide to Birds' Nests*. Boston: Houghton Mifflin, 1975.

Harrison, Kit and Hal Harrison. *America's Favorite Backyard Birds*. New York: Simon and Schuster, 1983.

Welty, Joel Carl and Luis Baptista. *The Life of Birds*. New York: Saunders, 1988.

Index

About the Author

Oliver S. Owen is a Professor Emeritus for the University of Wisconsin at Eau Claire. He is the coauthor of *Natural Resource Conservation: An Ecological Approach* (Macmillan, 1991). Dr. Owen has also authored *Eco-Solutions* and *Intro to Your Environment* (Abdo & Daughters, 1993). Dr. Owen has a Ph.D. in zoology from Cornell University.

To my grandson, Amati,
may you grow up to always
appreciate and love nature.
— Grandpa Ollie

PRETTY**CITY**LONDON
DISCOVERING LONDON'S BEAUTIFUL PLACES

SIOBHAN FERGUSON

The
History
Press

@prettycitylondon and all other contributing Instagram accounts
are operated independently and are not affiliated with, endorsed or
sponsored by Instagram LLC.

First published 2018

The History Press
The Mill, Brimscombe Port
Stroud, Gloucestershire, GL5 2QG
www.thehistorypress.co.uk

British Library Cataloguing in Publication Data.
A catalogue record for this book is available from the British Library.

ISBN 978 0 7509 8559 8

Design by Katie Beard
Printed in Turkey

CONTENTS

INTRODUCTION

London perpetually attracts, stimulates, gives me a play and a story and a poem, without any trouble, save that of moving my legs through the streets ... to walk alone through London is the greatest rest.

Virginia Woolf

London is a wonderful city: hectic, multi-layered, vibrant and fun, rich in history and home to so many of the world's most famous landmarks. From royal palaces to royal parks, from the finest museums to one-off art galleries, with new landmarks popping up all the time, you could literally spend days on end exploring and still always manage to find something new to see and do. It is no surprise that these landmarks make every 'must-see in London' list as they are, without question, truly spectacular. With their popularity comes crowds all the year round.

I remember my first ever visit to London, a quick weekend trip to visit a friend. I hopped off my flight from Ireland with a list a mile long of things I wanted to see and do, and I barely stopped for a second for fear of running out of time. I spent that weekend in endless queues trying to get a glimpse of the famous landmarks; I hopped on and off the busy Tube a million times, left tired but totally in awe of the beautiful capital. My next visit a few months later, and almost eighteen years ago, lasted a whole lot longer. I moved here to live and work and now, all these years later, I still call it home. Having ticked most of the landmarks off my list on that initial visit, and commuting into central London for work all week long, I found that when I was gifted with spare time I wanted to escape that noise, avoid the crowds and explore the gentle yet characterful side of the city.

Once I started exploring this side of London I simply couldn't stop; I found myself continuously drawn to its charming neighbourhoods. I quickly realised what Virginia Woolf had in mind when she suggested that a walk around London alone was a great rest. I quickly discovered too that beyond the big named tourist attractions lie beautiful and unique

village-like enclaves. I discovered that many of these hidden gems lie a stone's throw from the well-known icons. I loved exploring at my leisure, slowly and getting to know the people – people who inhabit them and contribute to their unique and individual charms and people who, like me, are drawn to these charming enclaves.

I started using my smartphone to capture moments from my wanderings around the capital; both the large-scale and the simple caught my eye. From cobbled street mews to the grand squares of Belgravia, from pretty bunches of peonies outside an Underground station to pink cherry blossom trees in Notting Hill. Once I discovered Instagram I started to share my captures, and I couldn't believe how popular this side of London was.

Wanting to embrace the community side of Instagram I created the hashtag #prettycitylondon and soon others started posting using the hashtag too. I decided to create a dedicated feed for @prettycitylondon. All the images tagged and shared on @prettycitylondon share a similar aesthetic, a beautiful romantic side of the city. Most images are captured in the city's neighbourhoods, these 'villages' bursting with charm and character with postcard-worthy scenes around every corner. Characterful independent shops, perfect mews, well-placed bikes, vintage cars and fairytale-like florists are the back bone of Pretty City London's aesthetic. Stylish Notting Hill, well-heeled Belgravia and leafy Hampstead all play lead roles. Some well-known central tourist spots star too, albeit their quieter parts.

This book aims to complement the Instagram feed and is a celebration of the beautiful places found all over the city away from the crowded touristy icons. It features a bucket list of itineraries and some helpful tips on how to capture and create your very own postcards of Pretty City London.

It is about the pretty, it is about the charm – but most of all it is about a London that is there for all to enjoy. There are no exclusive clubs; sure, it includes some of the most expensive neighbourhoods in the world, but it is to inspire you to explore and enjoy these without breaking the bank.

HOW TO USE THIS BOOK

The book is, for the most part, a visual celebration of the most beautiful places in London. It includes four key sections: photography tips, neighbourhoods, through the seasons and, finally, a bucket list of things to do in Pretty City London.

The book is intended to complement the popular Instagram feed @prettycitylondon, so will include many references to the social app throughout. Despite this, it is hoped that its visually beautiful content can equally be enjoyed by those of you not familiar with Instagram. It also hopes to inspire anyone either travelling to London or locals looking for spare time travel inspiration.

The photography tips section includes helpful tips on how to take beautiful Instagram captures to share with @prettycitylondon. The neighbourhoods section, as the name suggests, is arranged by the areas of the capital that truly represent the Pretty City London aesthetic and charm. Some areas are grouped together in one section, as to explore them together makes logistical sense and they have features that complement each other. This section also features a variety of locations worth visiting and easy to capture, from shops to cafes, galleries to parks. The larger areas contain a sample guided walk, while smaller areas simply list the streets to visit.

Through the Seasons is a short section celebrating the changing seasons in Pretty City London; finally, the bucket list section is a beautifully curated list of ideas of things to do in the city to truly experience the essence of Pretty City London.

The maps at the beginning of each section are an indication of what to expect in the area rather than to scale.

PART I

PHOTOGRAPHY TIPS

The @prettycitylondon Instagram feed is full to the brim with beautifully captured images of London, all with a similar aesthetic and vibe. The feed is primarily focused on the city's unique and characterful neighbourhoods, their residents and their visitors. Perfect façades, that well-placed bike, a charming shopfront, a pretty mews, florist or bakery all play a key role in the pretty city story. You will be pleased and perhaps surprised to learn that most of the shots shared on @prettycitylondon are actually smartphone shots. Most people carry one all the time so rarely miss a photo opportunity, and best of all it is extremely discreet. Below are some tips on how to get the most from it and capture the perfect shot worthy of feature on the @prettycitylondon page.

CHASE THE LIGHT

No matter the type of photography, light is essential to any great photo and natural lighting is simply the best. A smartphone can capture brilliant photos with ample light. I prefer to shoot on overcast days (London has a fair share) or otherwise during golden hour, i.e. early in the day or later in the evening. London isn't often associated with sun, but we do in fact get plenty of it and the days it arrives in all its glory are the hardest days to shoot in. If there is no cloud cover, seek out the shade and get the indoor shots out of the way in the middle of the day when it is at its harshest. In a nutshell, you should try and find that soft natural light, as it will make a significant difference to the result. If you are trying to capture a coffee or pretty breakfast scene and have to do so indoors, seek the table near the window and get snapping. It must be said that it is best to avoid direct sunlight through the windows, as that will give you the same problems as shooting in direct sun outside. Instead, seek that soft overcast light. Train your eye to find it; trust me, once you do you will never look at clouds in the same way again.

Fourteen
Trevor Square

HAVE YOUR CAMERA/SMARTPHONE READY AT ALL TIMES

London really is a photographer's dream and there is always something special to capture, be it a new bride walking down Portobello Road with her new husband yanking up her gown, or a beautiful vintage bike with a basket full of roses parked up outside a humble Chelsea cottage. Make sure to observe and be ready to capture. When I go to a particular area to shoot I like to seek that individuality that epitomises the style of the area, be it a quirky fashionista walking down Portobello Road or a quintessential British gent walking through Belgravia. I am forever on the lookout.

I love this capture by @truenord of a beautiful stranger walking barefoot through Greenwich Park with a beautiful bunch of balloons. The tone and colour palette is perfect for @prettycitylondon, but more than that I love that we are left guessing where this lovely lady is off to barefoot and fancy free. The inclusion of this lady in the frame adds an extra layer to the composition; true, the blossom alone would have been beautiful, but by including a person the photographer has added a little more depth to the image.

CHECK FOR THE DETAILS

The characterful neighbourhoods of London have stunning details in abundance: a pretty window, a colourful door, a floral arch or a vintage car parked in the right spot. That charming florist or those rowing boats along the Thames – they all need to be captured. Take your time, compose yourself and think about the story you want to tell through your image. If you have found the pretty façade you want to capture but would like to include a person, be patient and wait for the right person to enter the frame. London is full of quirky residents so you won't have to wait too long. Look at the entire frame through your view finder and try to eliminate obstructive subjects.

Think about colour as well. I like the softer tones to fill the feed and complement the current season; for example, Notting Hill and Primrose Hill really pop in spring and summer with their pastel houses, while you can't beat Hampstead and its cobbled streets for autumn/winter hues. Winter, and especially Christmas time, is Mayfair's finest season. Some areas are beautiful all year round; others have a season when they pop most.

PERSPECTIVE

Perspective plays a vital role in capturing the city. I come across plenty of wonderful images shared on #prettycitylondon with stunning compositions but the perspective is just not right. Step back from the taller buildings and get the horizons straight. Try to find a unique angle. Get creative with the parked cars, unless of course it's a nice vintage model. Instagram prefers straight-on shots for façades and shopfronts or top-down shots for food and coffee scenes. If you come across a nice composed scene, capture it at multiple different angles for sharing at different stages through your Instagram feed.

EDITING

The vast majority of images shared on #prettycitylondon have probably gone through some form of editing. While we all do it differently, it is important to find your signature style. Less is often or indeed always more. My favourite smartphone apps for editing are Lightroom for Mobile and VSCO (A6 or A5). Lightroom is fantastic for correcting light, colour balance and perspective, and VSCO to enhance the tone and give it that final pop at the end of the process. I don't follow a strict go-to editing process, but I do always play with a couple of basics in most of my captures. I like my Instagram images to be bright, crisp and clean, so I tend to pump up brightness, add a little contrast, play with the highlights and shadows and add a little sharpening sparingly. I typically add a small amount of VSCO Cam filter (A5/A6) at the end.

SHARING ON INSTAGRAM

So you have been using Instagram for a while and have figured out how it works; you now want to up your game a little and increase your following. Here are a few quick tips to make a difference:

- Think of Instagram as your portfolio, your way of letting potential clients see your work. A rule of thumb is to not over-share. Post regularly but don't overdo it; once a day seems to work well on most accounts.

- Try to develop a cohesive style with your images. If you are unsure what that style is, take a step back and analyse the photos you have taken and continue to take – do you see a pattern emerging? I am sure you will be surprised at how quickly you identify your own style. Settling on a theme or style can really help you beautify your feed.

- Plan your posts. There are many planning apps on the market; I use UNUM to plan my posts strategically, to see how they balance with one another. I like the colours and themes of my photos to complement one another.

- Use hashtags. Instagram hashtags are one of the best ways to grow your Instagram account. Using the right hashtag (or combination of hashtags) can help you expose your work to large and targeted audiences. In fact, your chances of attracting new followers, getting more likes, and increasing engagement are vastly increased by the use of hashtags. Popular and trending hashtags are a great way to develop your Instagram presence. Rather than use the common ones like #love or #cat, try something more relevant and meaningful.

PART II

NEIGHBOURHOODS

HOLLAND PARK,
NOTTING HILL,
KENSINGTON BORDERS
AND CONNAUGHT VILLAGE

A PERFECT BALANCE
OF ENGLISH GENTILITY
WITH BOHEMIAN CHARM

NOTTING HILL
& HOLLAND PARK

#prettycitylondon

SUMMERILL & BISHOP 100 Portland Rd
L MAISON 96 Portland Rd
CONNAUGHT VILLAGE Connaught St
ALICE'S 86 Portobello Rd

HARPER & TOMS FLOWERS Elgin Cres
WILD AT HEART 222 Westbourne Grove
JOHN & JESSIE 131E Kensington Church St

BISCUITEERS BOUTIQUE & ICING CAFE
194 Kensington Park Rd
PEDLARS 128 Talbot Rd
FARM GIRL CAFE 59A Portobello Rd

Clarendon Cross, Elgin Cres, St Luke's Mews,
Bathurst Mews, Hyde Park Gardens Mews

PRETTY CITY
LONDON

I am asked time and time again which is my favourite area to photograph in London, and I would have to say it is this one. In fact, I could have dedicated an entire book to this Instagram gem which lies just west of central London. From pristine pastel houses that span the area, to absurdly pretty mews, ethereal florists, vintage shops and pretty cafes, this area truly is the crème de la crème of Instagram destinations. It is the absolute backbone of Pretty City London. I would say the single biggest challenge I had finishing this book was resisting the urge to continue to visit the area gathering content. No matter the hour, day or time of year, a visit there always provides something new to find.

HOLLAND PARK

Suggested route:

Kick off your walk west of Holland Park Avenue at Royal Crescent and walk up through Addison Avenue; this tree-lined street is simply beautiful all year round, but, like so many others in this area, it truly pops in spring, with its magnolia and cherry blossom trees. Approaching Norland Square, you would be forgiven for thinking you had stepped back in time to the nineteenth century; this square, comprising stunning stucco-fronted houses and the odd vintage Minor is an Instagrammer's dream.

From here you can meander towards Portland Road and Clarendon Cross, where you will find a small crossroads of beautiful streets. This cluster of beautiful shops and fashionable residents provides a perfect insight to stylish neighbourhood life. It is anchored by the finest home shops, beauty parlour and cafe; you would be forgiven for thinking it had been airlifted from southern France. Always peaceful and yet with enough life to give it character, it is the perfect place to fill your camera roll with Insta-worthy images. It is difficult to believe as you admire the beautiful rows of pastel-coloured houses that these were once the site of slums, the 'Piggeries and Potteries', throughout the nineteenth century and it wasn't until the middle classes started to arrive in the 1970s that its beautiful Victorian properties were restored. It is a far cry from slum London today. I love to capture the happenings around the shops at its centre and refuel in the cafe of the beauty parlour, the Cowshed.

NOTTING HILL

After a mooch in the Cross shop or Summerill and Bishop, I suggest a slow stroll along Elgin Crescent towards the heart of Notting Hill, one of London's most stylish and vibrant areas. Stopping just before you reach Portobello Road on Kensington Park Road, you'll find one of my favourite flower stands in London, Harper and Tom's. After a stop to smell the roses, buy a bunch or take a picture continue left along Kensington Park Road where you'll find Biscuiteers, another of Pretty City London's famous icons. Stop here for a look around inside this very friendly and unique cafe. If you are after a perfectly iced biscuit souvenir or a stop for tea and biscuits, this is your place. In fact, this little stretch of Kensington Park Road is also home to many other great restaurants (many of them Italian) should you wish to stop for a bite.

MEWS IN THIS GENERAL
AREA WORTH SEEING

Codrington Mews

St Luke's Mews

Pembridge Mews

Bathurst Mews

Sussex Mews West

Holland Park Mews

Continuing on, I tend to cut across Portobello Road on to Talbot Road, passing and almost always stopping at Pedlars General Store, an Aladdin's cave of unique finds for your home and another perfect spot to refuel. A short stroll from here, just off All Saints Road, you'll find one of London's most iconic mews, St Luke's. In my opinion (and I believe I am not alone, given its popularity on Instagram) this is one of the capital's prettiest mews, made famous by its cameo in the blockbuster film *Love Actually*. I am always amazed that, despite its popularity, it is rarely that busy. Walk the length of the mews and back to truly take it all in. You'll have pretty pictures to last a lifetime after a visit to this mews.

Back out on All Saints Road and across the street from its entrance, you will find another gorgeous artisan cafe, the Tin Shed. Try their hot smoked salmon bagel (bagels baked on site every night) or Welsh rarebit – they won't disappoint. While they don't mind you taking photos, given its cosy size I would be mindful of other diners. Late afternoon during the week is a nice time to visit. It gets quiet, allowing you plenty of opportunities to capture its ambient interior.

From here, wend your way back to Portobello Road through Westbourne Grove, home to a plethora of designer shops, some great cafes and my very favourite florist in London, Nikki Tibbles Wild at Heart. With its array of seasonal blooms from hydrangea to peonies, it is impossible to walk by without capturing its beauty. After a wander along Westbourne Grove (take your time here, by the way) this stretch has everything. I potter back again towards Portobello Road until I come to Alice's. No visit to London would be the same without seeing Portobello Road, and if time is against you the section up from Gail's bakery towards Notting Hill Gate is my favourite. While it is heaving at the weekend, you will have a very different experience on a Monday. Thursday is my favourite day to stroll the road, as it is busy yet quiet enough to see it and breathe. Not far from Alice's, you'll find Farm Girl Cafe, a popular spot with fashionistas hoping to capture and fill their feeds with rose lattes; you may be one of the lucky ones to bag that courtyard table with natural light in abundance.

Continue on up Portobello Road towards Notting Hill Gate, and shortly after leaving Farm Girl you will find another beautiful stretch of pastel-coloured houses, my number one stop for that perfect stride-by.

GREEN SPACE

Hyde Park, Kensington Park
or Holland Park all close by

INSTAGRAM-FRIENDLY
HOTEL

The Laslett in Notting Hill

KENSINGTON BORDERS

If you have come to Notting Hill to find that perfect row of pastel houses, or indeed a quiet bite or lunchtime pint, but don't want the crowds that Portobello Road attracts then I would suggest a walk up to Hillgate Place and its surrounding streets. These rows of charming houses are all kept pristine by its private residents. This area is the perfect outdoor studio backdrop for those seeking to capture the perfect #ootd. Tucked away behind the busy tube station Notting Hill Gate, this little area is a true gem.

From here a little walk around the Kensington borders you'll find the Churchill Arms pub, one of London's finest, famed for its year-round floral arrangement. In the summer it overflows with pretty flowers and in winter with its spectacular Christmas trees and white lights. It is no wonder that any image of this gem is always well received on Instagram. From here you can explore the quiet off-road of Campden Hill.

CONNAUGHT VILLAGE

A brisk (half an hour or so) walk from Kensington Church Road through the periphery of Hyde Park towards Paddington, you will find Connaught Village and its neighbouring mews. My favourites are Bathurst and Hyde Park Garden Mews. Bathurst still runs some stable schools, which have been in use since the early nineteenth century. Walking through this L-shaped mews you'll feel the history oozing through the cobbled streets. With pretty houses and friendly residents, a walk through here is an absolute must. Close by lies Hyde Park Garden Mews, a must-visit in the summer months when its houses really up their window box game and you might be lucky to capture the horses from the nearby stables trotting by.

INSTAGRAM HOTSPOTS

Holland Park: Clarendon Cross/Norland Square and Addison Grove for shops; #bicichic and Cowshed for #coffeefliicks. Quiet stroll through the vastly residential area: hop over to Holland Park itself for a stroll through the park. Meander through Holland Park Mews on the way.

Notting Hill: Biscuiteers, Alice's of Portobello, Nikki Tibbles Wild at Heart, St Luke's Mews and Farm Girl Cafe. Hillgate Place for #ootd (outfit of the day) backdrop and that mint green figaro.

Campden Hill Road for stunning little cottages with rose floral arches.

Connaught Village: sleepy but charming area with plenty of beautiful mews to explore such as Hyde Park Garden Mews and Bathurst Mews. Connaught Street for stunning shopfronts as well as nice independent cafes and restaurants.

Kensington: you can't go wrong with a walk around here all year round. The Churchill Arms (the most beautiful pub in London), John and Jessie florists; this area is a must-see during #wisteria-hysteria season.

BELGRAVIA, CHELSEA, AND SOUTH KENSINGTON

QUINTESSENTIALLY BRITISH

KINNERTON ST

WILTON CRES

Rachel Vosper

MOTCOMB ST

THE THOMAS CUBITT

WINES SPIRITS

44 THE THO

Ottolengi

Alfred Tennyson

The Fine Cheese Co.

Baker & Spice

ELIZABETH ST

Poilane

The Thomas Cubitt

MUNGO & MAUD
DOG & CAT OUTFITTERS

PEGGY PORSCHEN
cakes

Mungo & Maud

EATON PL

EBURY ST

TomTom Coffee

Peggy Porschen Cakes

PIMLICO RD

Wild at Heart

B E L G R A V I A

#prettycity london

  MUNGO & MAUD 79 Elizabeth St
RACHEL VOSPER 69 Kinnerton St

  ALFRED TENNYSON 10 Motcomb St
THE THOMAS CUBITT Elizabeth St

WILD AT HEART 30A Pimlico Rd

  Kinnerton St, Eaton Pl, Wilton Cres

POILANE 46 Elizabeth St TOMTOM COFFEE 63 Elizabeth St THE FINE CHEESE CO. 17 Motcomb St
OTTOLENGI Motcomb St PEGGY PORSCHEN CAKES 116 Ebury St BAKER & SPICE 54-56 Elizabeth St

PRETTY CITY

L O N D O N

BELGRAVIA

Belgravia is beautiful, gentle and calm. Perhaps its reputation as one of the world's richest neighbourhoods puts tourists off descending on this refined area; it never seems overly busy, even though it is a hop, skip and jump from Buckingham Palace. Largely residential, its centrepiece Belgrave Square is serviced by three of the most exquisite streets in London: Wilton Row, Elizabeth and Motcomb. Its other artery, Pimlico Road, is equally stunning and charming.

As one of London's most exclusive neighbourhoods, it is hard to imagine that in the eighteenth century the area was a waterlogged wasteland and home to bandits and thieves. Gentrification took hold by the 1820s, when George IV developed Buckingham Palace, and the Grosvenor family who owned the area commissioned the builder Thomas Cubitt to turn it into the grand estate it is today. As I walk around the area it is mind-blowing

to think that the beautiful stucco houses as they still stand were the result of one master builder's work. Cubitt restricted building to exclusive private houses only, with smaller houses and public houses confined to the mews and smaller streets. This still holds true today.

Recently, thanks to the popularity of the Peggy Porschen cupcake parlour on Elizabeth Street and the Fine Cheese Company on Motcomb Street, Belgravia has become quite the mecca for the modern traveller or Instagrammer. Although the main draw to this enclave is its exquisite and elegant beauty, there is much more to it than aesthetic; as you walk around, it's hard to ignore the deep community spirit among its residents and shop-owners.

Suggested route:
I often marry a wander around Belgravia with a trip to Chelsea, so tend to start my walk around here with Pimlico Road; or, if I'm coming from the Victoria end, I start with a tour of Elizabeth Street.

INSTAGRAM-FRIENDLY
HOTEL

Artist Residence in Pimlico

GREEN SPACE

Green Park and Hyde Park

ELIZABETH STREET

As you leave behind the chaos of Victoria station, you have unmistakably arrived in Belgravia when you reach the intersection of Elizabeth and Ebury Street. You simply can't miss the bubblegum-pink façade of Peggy Porschen, the cutest cupcake parlour in the world. Expect a queue but don't leave; trust me, the champagne strawberry cupcake is worth the wait. With ever-changing decorations on display, friendly staff and exquisite cakes this really is a Pretty City institution. You may be lucky enough to bump into Peggy herself, the inspiring owner, and even luckier to learn of the parlour's history, influenced heavily by Peggy's own German roots.

Besides Peggy Porschen's, there is a lot more to explore for the eager Instagrammer; you will find the likes of Thomas Cubitt, florist Moyses Stevens, perfumer Les Senteurs, Poilane (delicious croissants), and Baker and Spice (excellent breakfast too) all lending themselves well to the perfect street-style

backdrop. My favourite lifestyle shop, Summerill and Bishop, have just opened a second shop on this street too. If you are not after a sweet treat from Peggy Porschen's then you can't beat a delicious brunch in the cosy but oh-so-perfect Tomtom Coffee House.

A stroll along this pretty street is a must; take your time, revisit, chat to the shop-owners. There are far too many cute cafes to try in one go.

PIMLICO ROAD

A mere five-minute walk from Peggy Porschen's you'll find Pimlico Road, known locally as a village, which is a must-see on any trip to our Pretty City. Here, fans of antiques and home shops can find some of London's finest. I like to just meander through it, chat to the locals, grab a takeaway coffee or bite from Daylesford and sit under a tree in Orange Square. I have

captured some of my most liked Instagram images here, mostly of Nikki Tibbles Wild at Heart florist. With buckets full of flowers all season long, you can fill #underthefloralspell aplenty. Head there on a Saturday for its fine farmers' market, and if visiting during the summer be sure to watch out for #BelgraviainBloom. This is typically the two weeks around Chelsea Flower Show, when most of the shops decorate their shopfronts with some of the finest floral displays I have ever seen.

MOTCOMB AND KINNERTON STREET

Two more charming shopping streets and home to quaint cobblestones and some of the most popular shopfronts captured for Instagram. The Fine Cheese Company on Motcomb and Ottolenghi is also simply beautiful to visit and capture. Follow the winding path off Motcomb down Kinnerton Street (with The Alfred Tennyson on its corner), and you'll find this perfect hidden gem which boasts some of the prettiest shops and English pubs in London. Step inside Rachel Vosper's shop and atelier for a real treat.

Other beauties include Egg Shop, which is more reflective of an art gallery than a shop – this space was once a dairy and still features the white barn doors.

INSTAGRAM HOTSPOTS

Pimlico Road: The Orange Pub, Rococo, No. 11 Pimlico Road, Artist Residence and all the residential streets leading off it for pretty houses.

Elizabeth Street: Jo Loves, The Thomas Cubitt, the annual village fete and the Belgravia Christmas Sunday need to be added to your diary.

Motcomb: Fine Cheese Company and Ottolenghi, The Alfred Tennyson.

Kinnerton: Clothes designer EGG, pubs and Rachel Vesper Candles.

CHELSEA

Walk down well-heeled King's Road today and many wouldn't believe that in the swinging sixties it was London's hippest street. I can believe it, however; while many of the independent boutiques of the late sixties have been replaced by global fashion chains, there are still plenty of inspiring fashionistas walking the streets. Outside of Instagram, it is renowned for being one of London's most affluent areas, with a plethora of posh shops and celebrity haunts, long since famed for its annual Flower Show which takes place in May. But within Instagram it is mostly associated with its beautiful and indeed quintessential and stereotypical preserved homes, a mix of palatial and humble properties, its historic book shop John Sandoe, cafe culture and the perfect place to add that chic #strangerinmyfeed capture.

CHELSEA

#prettycitylondon

 CABBAGES & ROSES 123 Sydney St

 THE REAL FLOWER COMPANY 13 Cale St
MOYSES STEVENS 188 Pavilion Rd

 GAIL'S BAKERY 209 King's Rd

 Chicama London 383 King's Rd

 Glebe Pl, St. Leonard's Tce, Bywater St,
Cheyne Row, Royal Ave

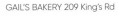 JOHN SANDOE (BOOKS) 10 Blacklands Tce

PRETTY CITY
LONDON

This pristine neighbourhood is the perfect place for a wander, and while the steep price tag might make the Chelsea Flower Show off limits, a complementary tour around the neighbourhood during the floral festival can be the perfect alternative. #ChelseainBloom is an annual event held to coincide with the Flower Show and it is free and open to all. I tend to focus my wanderings on the quiet side streets off the King's Road: Bywater Street, Chelsea Green and Leonard Terrace are all favourites of mine. Despite the number of excellent cafes and restaurants in the area, I typically visit Gail's on the King's Road (local artisan restaurants with fantastic selections of sweet and savoury delights) for a coffee and pastry or, for something more substantial, Chicama, a Peruvian-inspired Instagram delight, lies further down the King's Road.

Suggested route:

Alight at Sloane Square and head at your leisure towards the King's Road, a long street running from Sloane Square in the east to Fulham in the west. I tend to start my walk around the off streets to the right first. My first stop is always John Sandoe Book Store, an institution itself; established in the 1950s, stocked high with literary gems and flooded with light, upstairs and down, it is the perfect spot to capture.

From here, head back on to the King's Road for a short walk west to Bywater Street, a picturesque leafy residential cul de sac extremely popular today on Instagram for its row of pastel-coloured houses. Bywater is in fact the street that author John le Carré picked as the home for his fictional MI6 secret agent, George Smiley, in many of his novels. Behind Bywater you'll find the most charming village, Chelsea Green, tucked away from the bustle of the King's Road; a small enclave which is set around a little green common and has a great selection of shops, cafes and even a cheesemonger. I like to pop down here to the gorgeous florist, The Real

Flower Company, which is especially worth a visit during Chelsea Flower Show. Take a moment out with a sandwich from the deli, and sit in the green to watch the world go by.

Leaving Chelsea Green, I tend to walk towards the King's Road through Sydney Street. Stopping for a capture, mooch or shop at charming boutique, Cabbages and Roses, one of London's cosiest shops. With its understated florals and antique/washed-out colour palette, this beautiful fashion range embodies English Country at its very best. From here you can meander back up to the King's Road and choose to walk left or cross over the road and take a walk over to Oakley Street, the perfect spot to start your explore of the back streets of Chelsea. On Oakley you will find the insta-famous 'Love' door (pictured opposite). Don't leave the area without a walk around Cheyne Row, a hidden little cluster of picturesque cottages. They're a nice humble contrast to many of the 'palaces' you'll find in the most of the rest of Chelsea.

INSTAGRAM-FRIENDLY
HOTELS

Stay at nearby
South Kensington
hotels Ampersand
or Number Sixteen.

INSTAGRAM HOTSPOTS

Other must-see pockets of Chelsea include newly developed **Pavilion Road**, which runs parallel to Sloane Street and is home to a perfect selection of artisans and independents, with a butcher, cheesemonger and greengrocer all having pride of place among the retailers.

Smith Terrace, a pastel painted terrace street off the King's Road, with #bicichic and #asundaycarpic opportunities aplenty.

St Leonard's Terrace, a row of mid-eighteenth-century Grade II listed townhouses. Beautifully preserved and steeped in history, you'll find the former home of *Dracula* author Bram Stoker at No. 18. Don't miss this terrace during #wisteriahisteria season.

Duke of York Square, with a mix of original architecture and modern classic. You'll find plenty of restaurants and shops here, and you can visit the Saatchi Gallery for free.

GREEN SPACE

You can't get better than Chelsea
Physic Garden, founded in 1673,
situated on Royal Hospital Road.
It is a peaceful and calm oasis,
not free to enter but nonetheless
affordable.

SOUTH KENSINGTON

South Kensington, otherwise known as the Museum Quarter, with the Royal Albert Hotel, Natural History Museum, V&A and Science Museum all at its heart, coupled with some beautiful and affordable hotels, makes for the perfect place to stay in Pretty City London. Apparently a vast majority of London's French community live here, and it is often referred to as 'Paris's twenty-first *arrondissement*'. This chic and cultural hub of the city is popular on Instagram for its stunning stucco mansions, and indeed its picture-perfect mews around every corner. Exhibition Road is a favourite of mine for Instagram-friendly cafes, with Fernandez & Wells at its centre. It's busiest of course at the weekend; if you can manage an early morning weekday visit then you will be in for a treat.

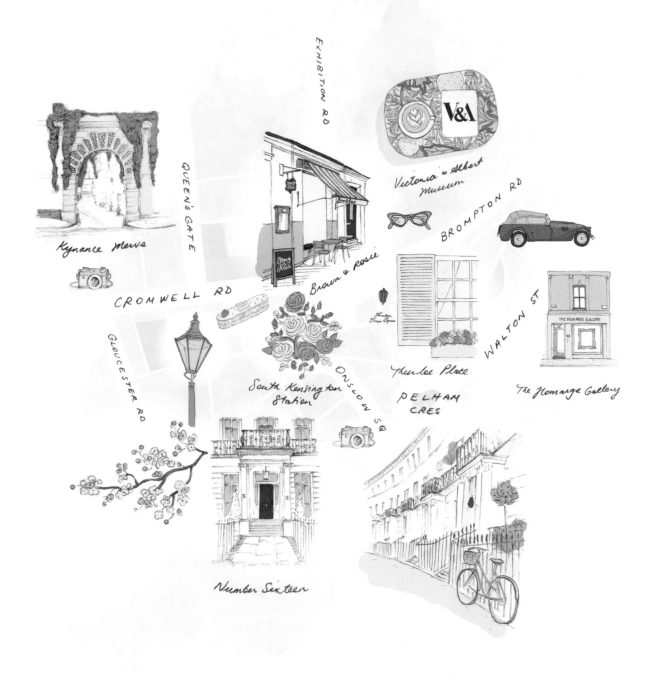

SOUTH KENSINGTON

#prettycity london

 VICTORIA & ALBERT MUSEUM Cromwell Rd
THE HOMARGE GALLERY 166A Walton St

 NUMBER SIXTEEN HOTEL 16 Sumner Pl

SOUTH KENSINGTON STATION Pelham St

 Kynance Mews, Pelham Cres,
Thurloe Square Garden

 BROWN & ROSIE 10 Exhibition Rd

PRETTY CITY
LONDON

Suggested route:

I like to kick off my visit to this area with a walk through one of my favourite mews in London; strictly speaking, this mews is not in South Kensington but rather just outside the South Kensington border near Gloucester Road. Hidden away between a pair of stone archways, Kynance mews is one of the most beautiful nineteenth-century mews in central London. It is best explored in autumn when its red leaves are in full bloom; however, it is true to say that a visit any time of year to this charming walkway, brimming with beauty and rich in history, is worth it. Although the area was heavily bombed during the Second World War it is incredible to learn that the mews itself survived unscathed. Walk through to be immediately transported to a fairytale-like pretty rustic village.

Following a trip to Kynance Mews I like to walk a short fifteen-minute stretch to the V&A Museum on Exhibition Road, the very best in Pretty

City London culture. Marry a mooch through the impressive art collection with a visit to the courtyard cafe or restaurant for the perfect Pretty City experience. The restaurant, housed in the original 'refreshment rooms', has the most impressive decor and architecture I have ever seen. Don't leave without a peep in the iconic museum shop (@v_and_a_shop) for a browse through the beautiful stationery range all wrapped with the inspiring and distinctive V& A pattern. I struggle to resist the urge to stock up on all things William Morris when I visit, but with souvenirs starting at as little as £1 there could be worse places to shop.

After a visit to the V& A, I tend to stroll down through Exhibition Road, on to Pelham Street, another charming street brimming with charming stucco-fronted houses set back from the street. From here I walk towards Walton Street, which runs parallel to Brompton Road; tucked away between South Kensington and Knightsbridge, this pretty strip is filled with beautiful independent shops and galleries. While they are not places for shopping

on a budget, they are the perfect place to browse and get a glimpse of West London charm. I am always drawn to the picture-perfect charming shopfronts and the chic passersby to add a little character to my images.

Leaving the charm of Walton Street behind me, I slowly walk towards Chelsea, meandering through Cadogan Square and Draycott Avenue and capturing scenes that catch my eye before settling for a while on Pavilion Road.

INSTAGRAM HOTSPOTS

V&A: culture, cafe and shop.
Kynance Mews: Nineteenth-century mews which survived the war; pretty cobbled streets, old brick façades, Wisteria vines and well-placed bikes.
Exhibition Road for Fernandez & Wells and Brown & Rosie cafe.
Gilding the Lily Flower Stand at South Kensington Tube, to fill your feed with beautiful blooms.
Pelham Street for stucco-fronted houses.
Walton Street for beautiful independent boutiques and The Enterprise pub.

GREEN SPACE

Nearby Hyde Park and
Kensington Gardens.

INSTAGRAM-FRIENDLY
HOTELS

Stay at Ampersand or Hotel Number
Sixteen in South Kensington.

HAMPSTEAD AND PRIMROSE HILL

ESCAPE TO THE ENGLISH COUNTRYSIDE
WITHOUT LEAVING LONDON

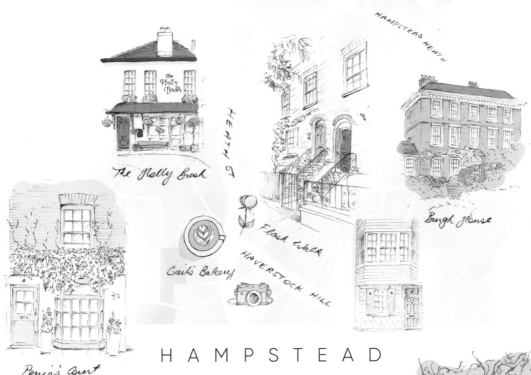

The Holly Bush

HEATH ST

Flask Walk

Gail's Bakery

HAVERSTOCK HILL

Burgh House

Perrin's Court

HAMPSTEAD

BELSIZE RD

Greenberry

REGENT'S PARK RD

Chalcot Square

L'Absinthe

Primrose Bakery

Chalcot Crescent

& PRIMROSE HILL

#prettycity london

PRETTY CITY
LONDON

HAMPSTEAD

Arrive at Hampstead Village in northwest London and you would be forgiven for thinking you have left London entirely, and ended up in the heart of the English countryside. Beautiful winding lanes, grand historic houses and humble Victorian cottages all nestled beside the heath make it people's number one choice to live in London; indeed, it is easy to see why it has long been hailed as 'the Jewel in London's Crown'. This hilltop hideaway has long been associated with artists and writers; take a slow stroll around this area to walk in the footsteps of the literary elite. Former residents include Sigmund Freud, Lord Alfred Douglas, George Orwell and Elizabeth Taylor, who no doubt moved here to enjoy the fresh air. To this day it is still popular among our stars, with Judi Dench, Sting and Ridley Scott, to name a few, all apparently having homes here.

Worth a visit:

Ignoring famous faces, stroll along the High Street, where you will spot many Grade II listed buildings. Although the street is lined with many chains, they blend in quite nicely. Veering off the High Street to one of its beautiful alleyways is a must. These winding lanes are home to some of the best independent and artisan retailers in the capital.

FLASK WALK

Quirky independents, a Grade II listed pub, the Flask, and beautiful florists line this cobbled street, making it a favourite on any pretty Instagram feed.

CHURCH ROW

Teeming with literary and artistic heritage, this eighteenth-century promenade is a sight to behold.

PERRIN COURT

This picturesque offshoot has plenty to offer, be it a coffee or bite. Local favourite Ginger and White is here. If you simply want to capture some street scenes, this is the place to be.

The climb to the Holly Bush is well worth it, too; this village local found in a beautiful back lane of the village is a great insight into former village life in the bygone era. If olde-worlde interiors are your thing, or capturing that al fresco drinking Londoners do so well, then head for this charmer. Around the corner from this quaint pub, you will discover a stunning view of the rooftops of Hampstead and the beautiful city beyond.

HAMPSTEAD HEATH

This is one of London's most beautiful open spaces, with 790 acres of grassy park, playing fields, swimming ponds and woodlands.

Burgh House and Hampstead Museum, a picturesque Queen Anne manor house dating back to 1704, complete with terraced garden, was lovingly restored in the late 1970s and today it celebrates the rich history of Hampstead Village. Over its 300-year history it has been home to everyone from local politicians to West Indian merchants. Don't leave without a visit to its basement buttery cafe for a hot chocolate or a slice of homemade cake.

PRIMROSE HILL

This picturesque village north of Regent's Park, once a very quiet pocket of London, is best known these days for its resident celebrities. Head straight for its beating heart Regent's Park Road for the crème de la crème of fine artisan cafes and independents, and a noticeable dearth of high-street chains. Although a little demure at times, it is without doubt extremely pretty.

Suggested route:
Walk across the bridge from Chalk Farm Tube and you are in pretty Primrose Hill. Lose an hour or two window-shopping on Regent's Park Road or sit outside an atmospheric cafe; Greenberry at the centre or Cowshed, which is located on the Chalk Farm end, are favourites with the locals. After a

mooch in the shops head for the beautiful Chalcot Square, former home of Sylvia Plath, or Chalcot Crescent, famed for, among other things, its part in the film *Paddington*. Capture the stunning pastel-coloured houses and their Insta-famous curve. After leaving there, walk along Chalcot Road – L'Absinthe, the village bistro, and the Princess of Wales, the village pub, are two Instagram gems and offer great options for food and drink. Don't leave without a visit to Primrose Hill Bakery on Gloucester Avenue; this retro-inspired cafe is worth the small detour from the main retail patch.

INSTAGRAM HOTSPOTS

Primrose Hill Books on Regent's Park Road, a family-run bookshop.
The Engineer Pub with garden.

INSTAGRAM-FRIENDLY HOTELS

Sadly this pocket of London is seriously lacking in good hotels, but less than 2km away you will find the exquisite Dorset Square Hotel in Marylebone (Firmdale Group of Hotels).

MARYLEBONE, MAYFAIR AND ST JAMES

HIGH-STYLE FAVOURITES

Moxon St

Daunt Books

Le Labo

MARYLEBONE HIGH ST

MONOCLE

THE MARYLEBONE

THE IVY CAFE

Monocle Café

PAUL ROTHE & SON

The Marylebone

The Ivy Cafe

WIGMORE ST

Aubaine

M A R Y L E B O N E

OXFORD ST

REGENT ST

Paul Rothe & Son

Taylor St Baristas

Liberty London

COACH AND HORSES

BOULESTIN

Mount St

Burlington Arcade

Canteen

Coach & Horses

PARK LN

PICCADILLY

F&M

Paxton & Whitfield

Fortnum & Mason

Boulestin

&   M A Y F A I R

#prettycitylondon

· PRETTY CITY ·
L O N D O N

MARYLEBONE

Just south of Oxford Street and north of Euston you'll find Marylebone, a pocket of London long famed for its fashionable shops. This remains the case today, with many of London's finest boutiques setting up shop there. Marylebone High Street, Marylebone Lane and Chiltern Street are all meccas for specialist shops and fine cafes. The plethora of high-quality shops and some of London's finest eateries attract an equally stylish crowd, making for some of the best opportunities to capture the perfect @prettycitylondon scenes.

Suggested route:
Hopping off the Tube at Baker Street, wend your way to Chiltern Street; the arrival of Chiltern Fire Station has put this beautiful street firmly on the 'stylish London' map. Home to some of my favourites from Cire Trudons

candles, Monocle Cafe and Trunk Clothing, this street is the perfect place to fill your camera roll with Instagram-worthy images.

Around the corner from Chiltern Street you'll find Marylebone High Street, with Daunt Book Store at its heart. Lose an hour or two in this former Edwardian bookshop; its long oak galleries and skylights make it a dream for both photographers and anyone looking for a travel guide.

Nearby Moxon Street is also worth a stroll to; here you will find Rococo Chocolates, La Fromagerie, the Ginger Pig and Instagram favourite The Marylebone pub.

After Moxon you can opt for a walk up to Devonshire Street, where you will find the perfume revolution that is Le Labo, inside the most aesthetically pleasing shop you are likely to see.

Turning back towards the High Street, end your tour of the area with a winding walk down Marylebone Lane, another mecca for stylish boutiques, cafes and small shops. V.V. Reuleaux, a destination in itself, is at No. 102, with Ivy Cafe and 108 Brasserie close by.

INSTAGRAM HOTSPOTS

Marylebone High Street, for Daunt Books and its side streets, Devonshire and Moxon.

Chiltern with the A-List mecca Chiltern Fire Station, Monocle and Trunk.

The Wallace Collection for its collection and cafe.

Paul Rothe & Son Deli established in 1900 with a beautiful shopfront still in place.

Marylebone Lane in general for pretty shops, cafes and street scenes.

INSTAGRAM-FRIENDLY
HOTELS

Stay at the Dorset Square Hotel.

MAYFAIR AND ST JAMES

Just west of John Nash's distinguished Regent Street, you will find the upmarket and high-style area of Mayfair. While most of the high-end galleries, restaurants and auction houses cater for the well-heeled and wealthy crowd, its elegant squares and quaint streets are most definitely worth a visit for a rich insight into London's historic retail past.

My favourite time of the year to explore this wealthy area is without doubt at Christmas; a walk through its beautiful arcades all decked in their finest for the season is a lovely way to spend a morning in the capital. My favourite arcade is Burlington, constructed in 1819, which runs from Piccadilly through to Burlington Lane. It is simply beautiful, from its supervising beadles in their traditional tall coats and top hats

(apparently there to ensure no whistling, singing or running through the arcade), to the array of beautiful mahogany-fronted shops, including Laduree and Penhaligons.

A short walk from here, you will find the smaller but by no means less pretty Royal Arcade, on Old Bond Street; its beautiful ceiling is a must-see for any Instagram and indeed non-Instagram visitors to the area. The opulent beauty doesn't stop at the arcades – the entire area is saturated with elegant sophistication. Outside of Christmas, I like to concentrate my wanderings around Jermyn Street in St James; although I'm not in the market for menswear, I'm still happy to window-shop, and there is no finer place for it. Floris, the oldest shop on the street, founded in 1730, Paxton & Whitfield Cheese Mongers and Fortnum and Masons are all my favourites.

GREEN SPACE

St James's Park and St James's Square.

INSTAGRAM-FRIENDLY HOTELS

So many to choose from, but @prettycitylondon loves the old-worldly charm of the Connaught.

INSTAGRAM HOTSPOTS

Shepherd Market: A charming small square enclave, with a variety of small shops, stylish boutiques cafes and pubs.

Wild Thing Flowers on Davies Street, one of the prettiest florists in London. St James, Jermyn Street for Fortnum's, Royal Arcade, Floris Perfumer, Paxton & Whitfield, Turnbull & Asser and Hawes and Curtis, all fine traditional shopfronts. Berry Bros. & Rudd and Locke and Co. on St James Street.

Pretty pubs of Mayfair: Coach and Horses on Bruton Street and its mock-Tudor with stained glass windows, and the Punch Bowl on Farm Street.

Liberty of London: Iconic emporium just outside Mayfair in Soho, it's worth a visit to see the exquisite mock-Tudor building for the beautiful window displays alone; step inside to mooch through the oak-panelled rooms spread over six floors. Don't leave without a stop at their fabric room, sipping a coffee in their cafe, a visit to the homewares section or a look at Nikki Tibbles Wild at Heart concession shop to the front.

COVENT GARDEN,
BLOOMSBURY
AND FITZROVIA

LITERARY SOPHISTICATION MEETS
BUSTLING MARKETPLACE

Warren Mews
Rebecca Hossack Art Gallery
WIGMORE ST
TAP Coffee
Sanderson London
CHARING CROSS RD
Charlotte St Hotel
RUSSELL SQUARE
Persephone Books
Bloomsbury Square
MUSEUM ST
Lamb's Conduit St

FITZROVIA & BLOOMSBURY

Murdock London
SHAFTESBURY AVE
7 DIALS
The Farthing
LONG ACRE
Monmouth Coffee
Neal's Yard Dairy
Ladurée
The Covent Garden Academy of Flowers
Covent Garden Piazza
STRAND
Taming of the Shrew
The Espresso Room
Laird Hatters
The Ivy
Mr Fogg's Tavern

COVENT GARDEN

#prettycitylondon

REBECCA HOSSACK ART GALLERY
28 Charlotte St

CHARLOTTE STREET HOTEL 15-17 Charlotte St
SANDERSON LONDON 50 Berners St
MR FOGG'S TAVERN 58 St Martin's Ln

THE COVENT GARDEN ACADEMY OF FLOWERS
St Martin's Courtyard

 Covent Garden Piazza, Lamb's Conduit St,
Museum St, Warren Mews, Bloomsbury Square

 LADURÉE 1 The Market
THE IVY 1a Henrietta St
MONMOUTH COFFEE 27 Monmouth St
TAP COFFEE 26 Rathbone Pl
THE ESPRESSO ROOM 24 New Row

PRETTY CITY
LONDON

COVENT GARDEN

Covent Garden, located in the heart of London and bustling with tourists, isn't a pocket of the capital immediately associated with Pretty City London but if you are lucky enough to visit it at its quiet moments – typically midweek – or are prepared to explore its side streets, it becomes clear why it is included here. A former fruit and flower market, it's known today for its quaint old arcades, Palladian-style piazza, amazing selection of shops, its many theatres and crème de la crème of street performers. Its piazza is certainly the star attraction, but a stroll around the small streets and alleyways that surround it have much to offer those seeking the best of London on a quieter scale. Of course, with all these pretty side streets come amazing Instagram opportunities.

academyofflowers.com
THE
COVENT GARDEN
ACADEMY
OF FLOWERS

Find the Pretty City in this neck of the woods by heading for Floral Street, a pedestrianised, cobblestoned thoroughfare, where you will find a mix of stylish one-off shops and boutiques.

A short stroll from here you will find New Row, a seemingly modern strip hiding a wealth of history. Originally built in 1644, it was used as the primary route for the market traders delivering the fresh fruit and vegetables to the market. Today you will find a few gems; Mr Fogg's Gin Parlour, decorated in 2017, with its floral arch, is a sight to behold in itself, but step inside the fictional home of the old globetrotter and you are going back in time to the 1800s. Gin lovers should head upstairs, where you will find a selection of over 300 different types. Also on this strip you will find other Instagram gems like Laird Hatters, a cap and hat shop; Hardy's Sweet shop, which celebrates the magic of the traditional English sweetshop; and New Row Coffee, a nice spot to refuel and capture #coffeefliicks.

Leaving New Row, head for Henrietta Street; unrecognisable today from its former self, it is now regarded as one of London's best menswear hubs. It also has recently opened a boutique hotel, Henrietta Hotel, attracting a stylish crowd. Aside from being a magnet for fashion-conscious men, it also is home to two of my favourite restaurants, Frenchie and Flat Iron. Cutting through St Paul's Church to King Street, which runs parallel to Henrietta, you will find some more Instagram gems in Aesop and Clos Maggiore, not to mention the much-anticipated and newly opened Petersham Nurseries. Lose an hour or two browsing this Insta-gold homeware and garden shop.

Don't leave without a walk around the main piazza, whether you simply grab a macaroon or two from Maison Laduree and sit on the steps to watch the free street performers, mooch through the market stalls or listen to the classical musicians, here is the place to capture a good slice of London. As I walk around I like to imagine what it was like as a bustling fruit and vegetable market; images of Eliza Doolittle and Prof. Henry Higgins, and people transporting baskets and barrels on their heads mull around in my brain. Of course, this is far removed from the Covent Garden of today; nonetheless it still has a bustling energy at its core. The iconic green arches of the Apple Market building are the perfect backdrop for any beautiful captures of this special place. I typically pick a quiet spot if possible and observe the atmosphere, trying to capture the vibe on camera.

This year has been especially lovely in Covent Garden, with their first ever installation at Chelsea Flower Show and the transformation of the piazza and its surrounds to celebrate its floral history. The silver-medal-winning Chelsea Flower Show garden has been transported back to the piazza and shops and restaurants of the area celebrated too with botanical window displays and exclusive in-store experiences unique to the area.

After a good long mooch around the piazza, head for more of the quieter side streets; I love Balthazaar on Russell Street for a late-morning coffee, or if peckish I like to grab a sandwich or pastries from its Boulangerie next door. Leaving Russell Street behind, I walk along Wellington Street, another street brimming with Instagram opportunities, from Penhaligons Perfumers on your right to a plethora of restaurants on your left. Tavistock Street is also great to capture/ soak up the cafe culture of the area. Cafe Murano is perfect for these scenes.

Worth a visit:

SEVEN DIALS

Once the hangout of bandits and thieves and poor street traders, Thomas Neal developed the area and its surrounds between 1693 and 1710. It has only become fashionable, however, since the gentrification of Covent Garden in the 1970s. Today it is the perfect place to soak up the atmosphere of London. Monmouth Street is one of my favourite streets in London to photograph. The cobblestoned street, lined with pretty coloured bunting, is home to many of Instagram's favourites, like Monmouth Coffee, Club Monaco and Murdock's barbers. Covent Garden Hotel is also there and you would find it hard to find a more picturesque façade. Part of the Firmdale Group, it's housed in a building which dates back to the 1890s – an old French hospital, hence the engraving '*Hôpital et Dispensaire Français*'.

SOMERSET HOUSE

On the site of a former palace, Somerset House is one of London's finest eighteenth-century buildings, with an impressive art gallery (Courtauld), an open-air atmospheric fountain courtyard, a terraced cafe and a host of other dining options. Its position overlooking the Thames and its neo-classical architecture is worth the visit alone. It is easy to see why this beautiful destination has provided the background to many Hollywood blockbusters and award-winning tv shows. I love to step inside its courtyard to truly escape the noise of the area – you could quite easily spend an entire day here. Have a picnic and settle in the courtyard; in winter months it is home to an impressive ice rink and in summer children can sprint through the beautiful fountains. Grab a coffee or bite from Fernandez & Wells or Tom's Kitchen, or visit Skye Gyngell's Spring restaurant for a special occasion. Capture the scale of two of the most beautiful sweeping staircases, Stamp and Nelson, in the South Wing.

CECIL COURT

This is a historic street which dates back to the seventeenth century, lined with beautiful shopfronts and linking Charing Cross Road with St Martin's Lane. Many of its beautiful bookshops feature in novels and films.

INSTAGRAM HOTSPOTS

Maidan Lane for Covent Garden Grind (coffee shots).
Bow Street for the bronze statue of the Young Dancer by Ezzo Plazzotta.
Neal's Yard, a centre for organic eating, is another photography gem.
St Martins Courtyard, urban oasis, new dining and shopping destination. It is worth a trip to see Covent Garden Academy of Flowers but note photographs are not generally permitted inside, so you should ask in advance.

BLOOMSBURY

Crossing Great Queen Street, and walking through Drury Lane, going north, you will arrive at Bloomsbury, an area quite often referred to as the academic heart of the capital. Developed by the Russell family in the seventeenth and eighteenth centuries, it is today home to the British Museum and University College. This pocket of London truly has the unmistakeable aura of an academic enclave; it was also home to many of England's most prolific writers in the early twentieth century, including Victoria Woolf and many other members of the Bloomsbury Group (members would meet regularly in the area to discuss politics, arts and others issues). Although this neighbourhood is best known among tourists for the iconic British Museum, there is so much more to the area than the museum. As you walk around it today, through its beautiful squares, you will find many of London's finest cafes and bookshops, an array of garden squares and elegant Georgian terraces.

SUGGESTED STREETS

Bloomsbury Square, London's oldest square, surrounded by historic period buildings and the grand façade of Victoria House, is one of the most beautiful places to visit in London. Bedford and Russell are equally stunning. Museum Street is a perfect thoroughfare for pretty cafes and classic shopfronts like Abbot and Holder Ltd and Thomas Farthing.

Lamb's Conduit Street, a partly pedestrianised street tucked away in Bloomsbury, is most certainly a hidden gem; although those in the know will have heard of it as a unique shopping destination, many tourists won't. Pop into Persephone Bookstore for a browse through lost classics by little-known female authors. This small shop flooded with natural light to the front is a beautiful place to capture, both inside and out. You can rehydrate at atmospheric Noble Rot or the Lamb (favoured in the past by local resident Charles Dickens) or get an understated coffee at Knockbox Coffee.

FITZROVIA

Fitzrovia, to the east, is a maze of leafy streets inhabited today by advertising agencies and creatives, but it hasn't always been so appealing. Once grubby and rundown and home to the underpaid artist, it wasn't until recent years that it has seen a beautiful revival with new restaurants, bars and cafes opening throughout. It is also home to some of London's – and indeed Instagram's – finest hotels, Charlotte Street Hotel and the Sanderson. Head to Charlotte Street Hotel to witness its beautiful façade for yourself or treat yourself to an Alice and Wonderland-themed afternoon tea at the Sanderson Hotel.

If nothing else, feast your eyes on one of @prettycitylondon's most popular subjects, Warren Street Mews, with its popular pink and green bikes parked outside Rebecca Hossack's home; peeping through its squared archway is like peering back through the ages. It is hard to fathom that Euston Road, one of London's busiest areas, is just a street or two away.

INSTAGRAM HOTSPOTS

Beas of Bloomsbury for pretty afternoon tea and cake.
Holborn Grind for the perfect coffee shots.
London Review Bookshop in Bloomsbury.
26 Tap Coffee in Fitzrovia.
Riding House Cafe.

INSTAGRAM-FRIENDLY
HOTELS

Charlotte Street Hotel.
Sanderson.
Covent Garden Hotel.
The Hoxton in Holborn.

CHISWICK, KEW, BARNES VILLAGE AND RICHMOND

BY THE RIVER

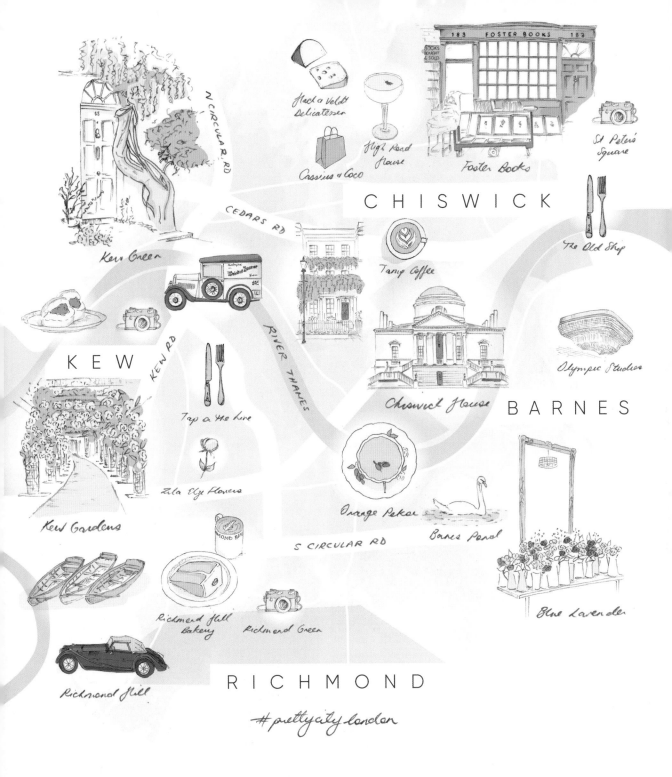

183 FOSTER BOOKS 183
BOOKS BOUGHT & SOLD

Hack a Veldt Delicatessen

High Road House

Cassius & Coco

Foster Books

St Peter's Square

N CIRCULAR RD

CEDARS RD

CHISWICK

Kew Green

Tamp Coffee

The Old Ship

River Thames

KEW RD

Kew Rd

Tap on the Line

Chiswick House

Olympic Studios

KEW

BARNES

Zita Elze Flowers

Kew Gardens

Orange Pekoe

Barnes Pond

S CIRCULAR RD

Blue Lavender

Richmond Hill Bakery

Richmond Green

RICHMOND

Richmond Hill

#prettycity london

PRETTY CITY
LONDON

CHISWICK

The upmarket Chiswick, a former fishing village, is today a lovely and quiet family-friendly pocket of the capital. A mix of Edwardian and Victorian homes and glorious green spaces are nestled beside a generous mix of cafes and independents.

Suggested route:
Walk along Turnham Green Terrace to find a plethora of interesting shopfronts and cafes to enjoy. Coffeehouse and deli Hack and Veldt, concept store Cassius and Coco, and deli Bayley and Sage are among my favourites. Around the corner on the High Street you will find High Road House, a local High Road brasserie; complete with stylish al fresco terrace and private members' bar upstairs, it is the perfect place to stop for a bite to eat. Next door to here you will find antiques emporium the Old Cinema, which is definitely worth popping into. Crossing over the road a little, walk to the right and cross over Devonshire Road to find Foster Book Store. This family-run bookshop has become a real hit on Instagram.

A couple of doors away lies No. 197, Chiswick Fire Station, an independent bar and restaurant with a beautiful garden. This Instagram gem, which is open all day long and flooded with natural light, is the perfect place to add to your #interiorgoals shots. From here you can choose to explore nearby Devonshire Road, which is lined with clothes shops, cafes and independents. Urban Pantry is nice inside and out and you will struggle to find better coffee in the area besides Tamp which is also great for #latteeart.

Looping back on to the High Street, I generally walk towards St Peter's Square, located in Hammersmith on the Chiswick borders. This 1820s garden square is surrounded by incredibly beautiful stucco-fronted houses, each with a grand porch. Stepping into this square is like stepping back in time. After a walk around the square and a stroll over to Black Lion Lane to see the likes of St Peter's Church, I wend my way north and under the underpass to the riverside, to walk the very pretty stretch of Chiswick Mall. Although popular with local joggers and cyclists, this area is still one

of the most beautiful and peaceful places to stroll, with boats, rowers and quaint pubs all along your path. You can choose to walk the entire stretch from Chiswick Mall to Kew Bridge but I typically veer off towards Chiswick House.

Chiswick House, a stunning neo-palladian villa set in beautiful historic gardens, with a contemporary cafe, is one of the most picturesque places in this area. The house was inspired by a love of Italy and built in the eighteenth century. The seasonal changes are pronounced with a stroll through the impressive grounds; enjoy a foggy morning stroll through and warm up with a cosy vegetable soup and crusty roll in the cafe afterwards. Watch out too for exciting events taking place in the grounds: open-air cinema in the summer months and dog shows in autumn, as well as open house events. The Camellia show in the Grade I listed conservatory takes place typically in early spring.

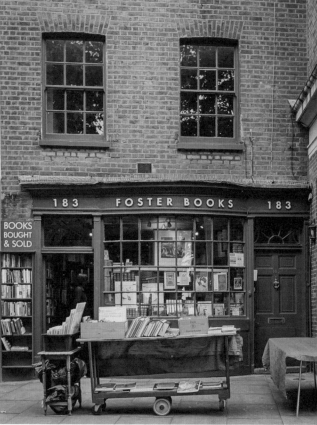

KEW

Follow a long morning adventure in Chiswick by a visit to Kew, another beautiful village in West London, best known for its Royal Botanical Gardens, Kew Gardens. The village and its nearby green are definitely worth exploring too.

Worth a Visit:
Rather than a suggested route for this area I will list the areas worth visiting.

KEW VILLAGE

A charming little village brimming with cafes, restaurants and independents. Oliver's wholefood shop, Tap the Line and Kew Green House are among my favourites to capture. Kew village also encompasses a stretch of shops on Sandycombe Road, one of which is a beautiful florist and workshop owned by Zita Elze. On the first Sunday of every month, between 10 a.m. and 2 p.m., the Kew village market takes place and the village streets are closed to traffic to make way for the bustling market.

KEW GARDENS

World-famous botanical gardens and centre of botanical science, brimming with precious specimen trees, the Pagoda, glasshouses, stunning vistas, historic buildings, shops, cafes, playgrounds, beautiful woods and a vast range of rare and beautiful plants. It is a sight to behold regardless of the season (there is a fee to enter but it is worth it).

KEW ROAD AND KEW GREEN

Exit Kew Gardens at Victoria Gate and walk along Kew Road to Kew Green, passing many Instagram gems such as the Original Maids of Honour, with a history dating back to Tudor times. Also along this stretch you will find some beautiful humble cottages.

Kew Green is a beautiful and vast open green common, lined with beautiful Edwardian and Victorian houses (some listed buildings). The eastern and south-western sides of the green are residential; the northern side is largely residential too with some pubs and restaurants. The Coach and Horses pub and boutique hotel is at No. 8 and definitely worth popping into. You can also opt to enter Kew Gardens from the green at Elizabeth Gate. The beautiful pond near the north-east corner of the green is also stunning to capture.

This area is beautiful all year round but I especially love it during wisteria season and summer, when you can capture it at its best. It lays claim to a wonderful summer fete.

As you leave the green, going back towards Chiswick and crossing over Kew Bridge, and walking back along the river, you will arrive at a lovely stretch known as Strand-on-the-Green, another beautiful albeit small riverside village rich in history. The grand homes we see today have been there since the eighteenth century, as have the pubs, the Bell and Crown and the City Barge.

INSTAGRAM HOTSPOTS

Kew village: Quaint and charming with a village vibe.
Zita Elze: Florist on Sandycombe Road.
Kew Gardens: Palm house and Kew Palace are Instagram gems.
Kew Green: The north side of the green during wisteria season.
Strand-on-the-Green: For grand houses and riverside ambience.

GREEN SPACE

Kew Green.

INSTAGRAM-FRIENDLY HOTEL

High Road Brasserie in Chiswick.

BARNES VILLAGE

Another picturesque riverside village worth visiting is Barnes, brimming with charm and that delicious village atmosphere. Think bunting, summer fetes, bonfire nights and boat race; yes, this quaint enclave has it all. Small enough to explore in a morning with little pretty scenes around every corner, one visit will leave you wanting to come back for more. The beating heart of the village is its picturesque pond, complete with ducks and geese. Like other Thameside villages it has plenty of charming cafes, village pubs and shops. My favourites are Orange Pekoe, on White Hart Lane, Gail's near the pond or the brasserie of the Olympic Cinema on Church Road. The river-facing Terrace is beautiful to capture too. Don't leave without a visit to the gorgeous florist Blue Lavender on Church Road and a wander down one of its many charming residential offshoots for the prettiest terraced houses.

INSTAGRAM HOTSPOTS

Orange Pekoe on White Hart Lane: For glorious coffees and a selection of teas to die for; for a special treat try their afternoon tea.
Barnes Pond: Especially lovely in spring when the wild flowers are in bloom.
Gail's Bakery: For artisan treats and coffee.
Olympic Cinema on Church Road.
Blue Lavender florist on Church Road.

RICHMOND

Perhaps my favourite of all London's riverside villages. Stepping off the train here is again like leaving London for the English countryside and perhaps even a bygone era. The peaceful village has it all, from grand houses to historic pubs, riverside walks, adorable cobbled alleyways, cafes and of course one of the most beautiful green spaces in the world, Richmond Park. Walking around it, it is so easy to see why Richmond was the favoured retreat for the royal court in Tudor times.

Suggested route:
Hop off the Tube at Richmond Station and head towards leafy Richmond Green, always full of village charm regardless the time of day or day of the week. After a stroll around here or a picnic on the grass, mooch in the shops along the hidden cobbled alleyways (Brewers Lane or Golden Court) or stop for a drink at the Cricketers. Pop into Aesop Skincare, housed in a beautiful Georgian house, or stop for a bite at No. 1 Duke Street. Meander slowly towards the river down through Water Lane.

Ahead of you to your right you will see the well-known White Cross pub, with enviable views over the Thames; turning left you can start your picturesque walk along the Thames. From here you can choose to walk the length of the Thames Path to Petersham Nurseries (about a mile). If you do indeed choose to do that you are in for a real treat. Petersham Nurseries, with its gorgeous rustic greenhouses, tea houses and award-winning restaurant, is the prettiest place on earth.

Alternatively, if you don't walk over to Petersham Nurseries you can start the climb up Richmond Hill towards Richmond Park, the perfect spot to capture fallow and red deer which roam the park freely. After a stroll through the park, head back towards Richmond through Richmond Hill. You can recover after all the walking at Richmond Hill Bakery, the perfect place for delicious homemade delights and excellent coffee. After your treats, you can start your descent back into Richmond village.

INSTAGRAM HOTSPOTS

Richmond Green, especially the stretch near the Cricketers pub.

Cobbled alleyway Brewers Lane.

Aesop on King Street.

Riverside walk from **Richmond Bridge** to **Petersham Nurseries**.

Richmond Hill bakery.

Richmond Park.

SOHO,
GREENWICH
AND
EAST LONDON

POCKETS OF PRETTY

SOHO

Words and images by Giulia Balleti of @giuliaballeti.

At first glance when thinking of Pretty City London, Soho is not the first place that comes to mind. But as you walk down Lexington Street, passing the candlelit windows of Andrew Edmunds and the pastel façade of Mildred's, you are transported to the romantic side of Soho. Located just below Carnaby Street, this small pocket of the West End could easily be missed by the unsuspecting tourist. And what a shame that would be, as there are some treasures that should not be missed. Here are a few of my favourite spots.

   With its inky black façade, Andrew Edmunds has been serving its seasonal English menu in Soho since 1986. If you are lucky enough to secure an outdoor table for a pre-dinner drink, you can watch the wonderful street scenes of Soho before enjoying the most romantic of meals.

Lexington Street boasts the original Fernandez & Wells cafe, which has a distinctly European feel. Inside its simple, beautiful interior, you can enjoy breakfast, lunch or in the evenings a glass of wine while sampling some of the Iberico ham that hangs in its windows.

My top tip for Mildred's is to arrive early. This popular restaurant serves internationally inspired vegetarian and vegan dishes. With its no-bookings policy, it is not unknown for the queue to snake down Lexington Street. It is well worth the wait, though, to experience their tasty and beautiful healthy dishes.

Today a contemporary art gallery, the lovely shopfront below was originally the home of gun- and rifle-maker John Wilkes.

Don't leave the area without visiting Lina Stores, a family-run Italian delicatessen that sells the most delicious authentic Italian food.

GREENWICH

Words and images by @georgianlondon.

Greenwich is one of those parts of London where it is easy to forget that you're in the middle of a big city. It has a real village feel to it and a long maritime history – many people take a ferry to Greenwich from central London to make the most of its riverside location. Its large park is perfect for picnics in the summer and it has a pretty, historic town centre, full of quaint streets and with some lovely old houses and pubs. Some of the best places to visit include:

The covered market: open every day and showcasing craft and design stalls, as well as a variety of food stalls, it's lined with independent shops, pubs and bars.

The Queen's House: built in the seventeenth century, this former royal residence is now used by the Maritime Museum to display some of its art collection. It also has one of London's prettiest spiral staircases, the Tulip Stairs.

Old Royal Naval College: this World Heritage site is worth a peek, if only to visit (for free) the Painted Hall with its incredible baroque ceiling.

The upper part of Greenwich Park beyond the Royal Observatory: in April/May this is one of the best spots in London to view avenues of pink cherry blossom trees. Pop in to the Pavilion Cafe nearby for lunch or afternoon tea.

Croom's Hill: this street bordering Greenwich Park is full of stunning Georgian townhouses, one of which houses the Fan Museum, a small quirky museum with a beautiful orangery that serves cream teas in a lovely mural room overlooking a secret garden.

Hyde Vale nearby has some stunning houses, which are worth a visit, especially during wisteria season in spring, when they're covered in beautiful purple flowers.

Royal Hill: a stroll along this street is a must. The Creaky Shed is the prettiest greengrocer in London, with a name to match, and there are several lovely old pubs – the Greenwich Union and the Richard I are side by side and well worth a visit.

Trinity Grove: it's a little bit of a walk, but it's the quintessential pretty London street – pedestrianised and lined with cute houses (one with flowers growing in a bathtub outside!), and plenty of flowers and greenery. Visit in July/August when the street is strung with bunting; it's picture-perfect.

London is most certainly a city of seasons, a city with four distinct seasons (often all in one day), but while the weather can be unpredictable in this vibrant city there are certain images associated with the changing seasons that you can count on. From blossom in spring to the Chelsea Flower Show in summer with long summer evenings al fresco, from cosy pubs and crunchy leaves in autumn to the magical lights of Christmas in winter, each season has something spectacular to offer in Pretty City London.

EAST LONDON

Words by @sophia.gb; images by @sophia.gb and @siobhaise.

'Pretty' and 'East London' in the same sentence may feel like a contradiction, and although it lacks the manicured gardens of West London, there's still prettiness and charm to be found – assuming you know where to look. Saturdays are best spent grazing the Broadway Market food stalls and lounging in London Fields (weather permitting). Climpson & Sons is always my first stop for a caffeine fuel up! Sundays, if you're in the mood to brave the crowds, are for loading up on blooms at Columbia Road. Be sure to wander the side streets to find colourful doors and cute vintage cars. Meandering through Spitalfields transports you back in time, enjoy the well-maintained Georgian façades of Fournier and Prineclet street bookended by the quintessential stop for curry on neighbouring Brick Lane. Another colourful must-do is the lattes at Aida – rose, turmeric or matcha, or all three for a pastel, caffeine-filled array! Walk off the drinks on Redchurch Street, and be sure to stop in Burro e Salvia for the best home-made pasta if you're peckish.

PART III

PRETTY CITY LONDON THROUGH THE SEASONS

SPRING

It is spring. Thank heavens. It is typically summer that everyone looks forward to, but spring is definitely Pretty City London's finest season, largely due to the beautiful blossom growing everywhere. Cherry blossom season can begin as early as February, with the beautiful magnolia trees among the first to pop. Cherry blossom quickly follows, but it is when the wisteria arrives in early April that the magic of spring is well and truly evident in the capital. Soft purple petals climb over buildings all over Pretty City London.

You are likely to find blossom growing in any one of London's neighbourhoods but here are some tips on where to be guaranteed the best of it:

February	March to early May	April with second softer batch in late June
Magnolia	**Cherry Blossom**	**Wisteria**
St Mary Le Strand	St. Paul's Cathedral	Kew Green
Northumberland Road in Notting Hill	Greenwich Park: blossom avenue	Richmond Green
Kenwood House	Kew Gardens: cherry walk from the the King Williams Temple to Temperate House	Chelsea St Leonards Terrace

SUMMER

June, July and August are the months most people look forward to. Sun, warmth, al fresco dining during long summer evenings ... but it can be London's busiest time of year and sadly not the best in terms of sunshine. Nonetheless, we can't argue with its beauty. Everything pops, blossom trees make way for window boxes, village pubs compete with grand stucco houses for the best-dressed prize. It is also the season of Chelsea Flower Show, and #chelseainbloom and #belgraviainbloom, which see the beautiful shops of London transform their shopfronts with floral displays to die for. It is also a time for picnics in our beautiful parks – parks with plenty of trees to duck under should the weather dictate.

Embrace Summer in Pretty City London:

Summer Picnics: Any of our beautiful parks with St James's and Richmond Park being a favourite for summer.
#chelseainbloom and **Chelsea Flower Show**.
Covent Garden summer festivities: Always something special on, from pop-up champagne tents to floral festivals.
Visit the annual **Serpentine Pavilion**: every year since 2000 the gallery has commissioned a temporary summer pavilion.
Visit **Regent's Park** open-air theatre.
Run through the fountains at **Somerset House**.
Visit the rose gardens and pergola at **Kew Gardens**.

AUTUMN

Ironically some of our best weather in the capital comes in the early days of autumn when the children return to school. Temperatures can soar and, before you know it, crisp autumn days creep in. It is a very pretty time of year for London. The landscape, especially in our beautiful parks, changes from green to gold and stunning conkers line our paths. Grab a sweater and some boots and embrace the season.

Head to the parks where the crunchy fallen leaves transform the ground to a golden carpet and woodlands glow.

Some of London's neighbourhoods are best visited in autumn. I love to go to **Hampstead** or **Richmond** at this time of year when the golden hues suit their architecture so well.

Celebrate Halloween and take a neighbourhood walk to see some of the finest houses transformed for the spooky festival. **Chelsea**, **Notting Hill** and pockets of **Chiswick** are the best places to witness the crème de la crème of Halloween decorations.

Find a cosy pub; the **Audley** in Mayfair or the **Holly Bush** in Hampstead are the perfect spots for an autumn afternoon enjoying warm cider.

WINTER

With summer crowds and autumn behind us, London begins to exude a slightly different charm in winter, particularly at Christmas. With pantos, Liberty's Nut Crackers, Oxford Street and Regent Street lights, and Fortnum & Mason's whimsical windows, there is no finer place to celebrate the holiday season.

Embrace Christmas in Pretty City London:

Attend the **Christmas switch-on** at one of the various venues across London. My favourite is always **Covent Garden**. In 2016 it was more stunning than ever, when artists from the Royal Opera Chorus and Royal Ballet put on a truly spectacular show in the piazza.

Go window-shopping through **Mayfair**; head for its many stunning arcades to see the best of the festive decorations.

Visit the finest hotels of Mayfair to see their grand Christmas trees. **The Savoy** and **Claridge's** have particularly beautiful ones year on year. You may even be lucky enough to see Santa Claus.

Step into **Liberty's** or **Fortnum & Mason's Christmas shop**.

Take a walk down **Regent Street** and maybe even step on to **Oxford Street** to see the magical Christmas lights.

Go ice-skating at the **Natural History Museum** or **Somerset House** pop-up rinks.

Visit the **Winter Garden** at the Landmark Hotel.

Meander through **Chelsea** and **Belgravia** to enjoy the spectacular festive wreaths hanging on the pretty doors.

PART IV

BUCKET LIST OF THINGS TO DO IN PRETTY CITY LONDON

Assuming you have ticked the main Pretty City London spots off your list, here is a curated guide of the best things to do in the capital to experience London at its absolute best, brought to you by @prettycitylondon's local Instagrammers.

VISIT SOMERSET HOUSE

Words and images by Robin Hendrie of @sixsevensix.

For me, Somerset House is undoubtedly one of London's hidden gems. A quick visit can be both a calming and inspiring experience, and I find it to be the perfect location to take a moment to recharge and reset. Walking through the arches into the grounds of Somerset House from Westminster's bustling Strand, you are immediately struck by the size and grandeur of the building.

Entering the Upper Terrace, you find a wonderful view of Fountain Court; its iconic fountains entertain children in the warmer months and look particularly stunning with its ice rink and giant Christmas tree over the festive period. Here you can wander, take in the wonderful neo-classical architecture or, as I do, grab a flat white and a croissant from one of the cafes, sit back and partake in a spot of people-watching. I usually stop by Fernandez & Wells for coffee. Situated in the East Wing, you can sit inside the cafe or al fresco in the courtyard, but the window seats inside provide great light for that perfect Instagram coffee shot!

Alternatively, in the New Wing you'll find Pennethorne's, where you can enjoy a coffee or, if you prefer, a refreshing mix of beers, wines and contemporary cocktails. Taking its name from Sir James Pennethorne, the nineteenth-century English architect who designed the wing, the venue is an ode to his travels throughout Europe; with its high ceilings, rich dark walls, marble bar and brass-topped tables it's a far more elegant and impressive surrounding for drinks and nibbles.

PICNIC OUTSIDE

If the sun shines, grab your picnic blanket and basket and indulge in the very beautiful experience of enjoying a lovely picnic in one our beautiful parks: St James's, the park stretching along the Mall; Hyde Park, with views of the Serpentine; or Richmond Park, to spot the deer or on the top of Primrose Hill with views over the city.

Take a picnic and friends and head for the Isabella Plantation in Richmond Park, which provides one of the best shows of rhododendrons and azaleas in London (the flowers are at their best end of April/early May).
Regent's Park is an equally stunning park to enjoy a picnic. With its royal park status and views over the lake, it truly is the perfect spot for a picnic.

ENJOY AFTERNOON TEA

London has long been associated with afternoon tea and it is obvious why: there are just so many different venues to choose from. www.afternoontea. co.uk is an excellent reference and I have cherry-picked my favourites in London.

Fortnum & Mason in Piccadilly: expect eau-de-nil china, crisp white linen and delicious finger sandwiches and fluffy scones with a vast selection of teas on offer.
Biscuiteers in Notting Hill: less formal and more fairytale. Enjoy tea at this icing institution, all served on beautiful red-and-white-striped tableware outside or inside the cafe. A table outside, if weather allows, is best for getting your perfect Instagram capture.

Ampersand Hotel in South Kensington: enjoy a science-themed tea in the exquisite drawing room, perfectly stylish without being too formal.

Aubaine in Selfridges on Oxford Street: tucked away beside the Shoe Gallery in Selfridges you will find this cosy little nook, perfect to enjoy afternoon tea.

Laduree in Covent Garden: enjoy some delicious macaroons and pastries on the Parisian-style balcony overlooking St Paul's Church and the west piazza. Listen to the street performers while sipping tea with friends for the perfect Pretty City London experience.

Pret-a-Portea at the Berkeley Hotel in Knightsbridge: enjoy a leg+endary designer afternoon treat.

TREAT YOURSELF TO COFFEE AND CAKE

Don't fancy the indulgence and grand affair of an afternoon tea? Why not enjoy a simple coffee and cake instead, in one of our favourites.

Peggy Porschen in Belgravia for the ultimate Pretty City London experience: ultra feminine and oh-so-pretty it is the crème de la crème of pretty cafes in London. Try the Victoria sponge or Eton mess with floral rose tea.

Farm Girl Cafe on Portobello Road in Notting Hill: with its cult following it can be hard to get a place in the coveted courtyard, but if you are lucky then sit back and enjoy your rose lattes and acai bowl away from the bustle of Portobello Road market for a little while.

Rail House Cafe: If you want to fill your Instagram feed with pretty yet rustic coffee shots then head for this pretty cafe near Victoria station. With an airy and light aesthetic, inspired by train carriages, and beautiful

bespoke furniture, married with delicious food, you can't beat a visit to this cafe.

Other pretty cafes to try are **Hoxton Bar and Grill** in Shoreditch, **Drink Me Eat Me** in Hammersmith and **Fait Maison** near Gloucester Road Tube station.

FIND A PRETTY RESTAURANT
IN A GARDEN CENTRE

With London's weather so unpredictable it might be safer to opt for that indoor garden feeling. My favourites, without doubt, are Petersham Nurseries in Richmond and Clifton Nurseries in Little Venice. Both offer high-quality stock complemented by wonderful cafes and restaurants.

TRY A FRAGRANCE-PROFILING SESSION

Perfumer Penhaligon's offers a fragrance-profiling session in some of its most beautiful shops; you can choose from Wellington Street or Burlington Arcade. Spend a glorious half hour experiencing their one-on-one scent-profiling session and be matched to your perfect Penhaligon's fragrance.

WATCH THE STREET PERFORMERS IN COVENT GARDEN

Take a moment and sit in the Piazza in Covent Garden with an ice-cream or macaron from Laduree while enjoying the wonderful street performers.

EXPLORE COLUMBIA ROAD
AND ITS FLOWER MARKET

Embrace the crowds – or try your best to avoid them by getting to the market extremely early on a Sunday. This strip is like stepping on to a film set complete with chocolate-box shopfronts; it provides the perfect insight into what east London looked like under Queen Victoria's rule. Note that some of the shops only open on market day, so it is best to check before you visit. Its hard to pick a favourite shop, but after stepping into Bob and Blossom, a cute children's shop, I was pretty smitten.

EXPLORE PRETTY MEWS OF LONDON

Step back in time by visiting one or all of London's prettiest mews. There are plenty of these cobbled byways to explore, most built in the seventeenth and eighteenth centuries for equestrian use. Today they are home to many pretty houses. There are so many to visit in the city but South Kensington, Notting Hill and Paddington have the lion's share.

CHELSEA IN BLOOM

Not willing to join the queue for much-sought-after Chelsea Flower Show tickets, but wishing to enjoy its vibrant charm? Don't worry; just head to Chelsea while it is on to enjoy the free alternative Chelsea in Bloom festival.

WINDOW SHOP IN MAYFAIR

There is no doubt that Mayfair houses many of London's most exclusive boutiques, arcades and department stores, but even if you are not in the market for a Prada handbag you can still have a wonderful window-shopping spree here.

CONTRIBUTORS & ACKNOWLEDGEMENTS

All images © Siobhan Ferguson except:

@aglobetrot: p. 174

@ameliathecav: pp. 13, 26, 33

@angrybaker: pp. 4, 179, 182 (bottom right)

@belleannee: p. 184

@bobandblossom: p. 216 (bottom left)

@clairemenary: p. 215 (top)

@crazycatlady: p. 200 (top right)

@elenasham: pp. 187, 188, 189 (top left)

@francesmehardie: pp. 190, 191 (bottom left)

@georgianlondon: pp. 168, 169

@giuliabaletti: pp. 163, 164, 165 166

@hannahargyl: p. 182 (top)

@humphreyandgrace: p. 176 (top left and right)

@kseniaskos: pp. 179 (left), 198, 204 (bottom right), 206, 208 (top left), 223 (top right)

@sabzwong: p. 211 (left)

@sixsevensix: pp. 194, 196

@snowflaskesfairy: pp. 192, 193

@sophia.gb: pp. 171, 173

@steffi-daydreamer: pp. 185, 186

@truenord: p. 18

@kseniaskos is a spatial and graphic designer and is studying for an MA in Narrative Environments in Central Saint Martins. She felt in love with photography with her first camera when she was a teenager. Ksenia calls herself a visual storyteller, because she loves to take and post pictures with interesting stories, especially with beautiful strangers.

Julia, **@humphreyandgrace,** is a photographer and avid Instagrammer. She is based in East Sussex and travels to London regularly for work, often capturing scenes from London's residential areas between meetings. Julia has been Instagramming almost daily for over four years and writes a photography and lifestyle blog at www.humphreyandgrace.co.uk which includes several resources for improving your photography. She also loves a good floral ...

Mendy Waits, **@angrybaker**, is an American mom, carb addict, and lover of the local side of London life.

Jessica Lemaitre, **@snowflakesfairy**, is a photographer based in London. She first joined Instagram in 2013 and has documented her travels to twelve different countries.

Holly Webber, **@_hollywebber_**, is a graphic designer, art director and illustrator based in Tasmania, Australia, who graduated with a Bachelor of Fine Arts from the University of Tasmania in 2004. She has spent over a decade building up her design practice, gaining a diverse portfolio with experience in all areas of communication design for small and large businesses. Although she lives 10,000 miles away, Holly is no stranger to London. With family in the UK, she's a frequent visitor and loves exploring new parts of the city. She spends her time wandering the streets, admiring the architecture and surrounds. Holly can often be found in a cafe sipping on a long black, sketching scenes from her latest travels. Her website is at www.hollywebber.com.au.

Jessica Bride, **@belleannee**, is a New Orleanian food writer, blogger and social media photographer who lives in London with her husband and three children. She chronicles her life in the city, and travels beyond, through recipes, photographs and essays, She can often be found wandering Portobello Road in the heart of Notting Hill.

Giulia Baletti, **@giuliabaletti**, grew up in Australia. From a young age she wanted to explore the world, and as soon as she arrived in London she felt at home. With an architect for a father, she has always been passionate about interiors and design. Instagram has provided the opportunity to share those passions alongside her love for photography and street style. Through her images she tries to share her view of the London that she has come to know and love, giving back to a community that has given her so much. One of the greatest and most surprising gifts has been the opportunity to meet so many kind and inspiring creatives, many of whom will remain her friends for life.

Steffi Crivellaro, **@steffi_daydreamer**, is an adopted Londoner with a passion for photography and travelling. She also posts on @housesofldn and @welovetobrunch, where she created a community for people sharing the same interest as her and @roselladegori: great brunch and photography.

Claire Menary, **@clairemenary**, is a photographer based in London who shares stunning shots of everything from food, interiors, fashion and beauty.

Robin Hendrie, **@sixsevensix**, shares stunning lifestyle shots of London on his Instagram feed.

Sophia, **@sophia.gb**, is a former Londoner now living back in her native San Francisco. Her love of doors, architecture, and pastels is evident in her feed, as is drive her to explore cities across the globe. She sorely misses London, and is excited to share a few charming spots in East London!

Elena, **@elenasham**, is a London-based travel and lifestyle photographer. She has always lived in big cities and this is where she finds inspiration for many of her shots. Elena loves visiting new places, and finding new flavours – whether in a big city halfway across the world or an unvisited street within walking distance of where she lives.

Hannah Argyel, **@hannahargyle**, is a professional photographer living with her family in Northampton. Her website may be found at www.hannahargylephotography.com.

Skye O'Neill, **@georgianlondon**, is a London-based Instagrammer and blogger at skyeoneill.com. Working in publishing and with two young children, Skye fell into photography via Instagram. Passionate about London and all it has to offer, she is happiest when exploring the city and discovering hidden gems.

Sabrina, **@sabzwong**, is Malaysian-born, partly Msia/Indo/HK but mostly Aussie bred; she lives in London and loves food, travel and taking photos of pretty and interesting things while out and about!

Ashley Nordsletten, **@truenord**, is an unwitting US–London transplant and aspiring academic who, when not buried under books, enjoys wandering the wen and stumbling into the small stories that spring up in the 'big smoke'.

@francesmehardie is an Edinburgh girl based in London, www.hardieandwilder.com.

@crazycatlady is a London-based Instagrammer originally from Scotland.

ACKNOWLEDGEMENTS

Thank you to Noel and my boys, Jack, Charlie and Louis, for their endless love and support during this project.

Thank you to all the wonderful contributors, especially Holly Webber, for her perfect interpretation of my brief on the maps for @prettycitylondon.

Thank you to all my followers on my Instagram accounts, for your continued support and contribution to #prettycitylondon, and finally to all the unique and charming, shops, florists, cafes, restaurants and hotels that continue to make this city so very very pretty.